No Flour

Easy Clean Eating Recipes for Weight Loss and a Healthier You

Madison Miller

Copyrights

Disclaimer and Terms of Use

Effort has been made to ensure that the information in this book is accurate and complete. However, the author and the publisher do not warrant the accuracy of the information, text, and graphics contained within the book due to the rapidly changing nature of science, research, known and unknown facts, and internet. The author and the publisher do not hold any responsibility for errors, omissions, or contrary interpretation of the subject matter herein. This book is presented solely for motivational and informational purposes only.

The recipes provided in this book are for informational purposes only and are not intended to provide dietary advice. A medical practitioner should be consulted before making any changes in diet. Additionally, recipe cooking times may require adjustment depending on age and quality of appliances. Readers are strongly urged to take all precautions to ensure ingredients are fully cooked in order to avoid the dangers of foodborne illnesses. The recipes and suggestions provided in this book are solely the opinion of the author. The author and publisher do not take any responsibility for any consequences that may result due to following the instructions provided in this book.

ISBN: 978-1544021409

Printed in the United States

— THE —
COOK BOOK
PUBLISHER

Avant-Propos

If your goal is to be healthier this year, then you need a plan that is actually going to work. One of the hottest and most realistic diets today is the No Sugar No Flour plan. This diet promotes the consumption of whole, natural foods that contain no refined, simple carbohydrates. Different from low carb diets of the past, this diet takes out the struggle of complicated calculations and food lists, and replaces them with good old common sense. This cookbook illustrates just how delicious and incredibly varied your diet can be while following the No Sugar No Flour diet principles. From breakfast all the way to dessert, this book will carry you through and help you discover delicious new ways to meet your new dietary goals.

Contents

Introduction

Fad diets are no new thing. For decades, we have turned to countless new ways of eating in hopes of regaining our health and a more comfortable weight. The sad news is that an overwhelming number of fad diets fail in the long term. This, as you likely know, is because most dietary fads just aren't practical for real life. I have another theory that goes along with this. I feel that part of the reason most diets is fail is because few of them really address the underlying issues that have lead to a declining state of health while contributing to an increase in obesity rates. If you want to know where the root of the problem is, you need look no farther than your local grocery store.

When you walk into your grocery store, do you find that the perimeter of the store contains fresh meat, dairy, and produce, but the interior of the store, which encompasses the most space, is filled with products that have been processed and manufactured from ingredients that are neither natural nor wholesome? These aisles take up the most space because this is where the average consumer spends the most, and unfortunately this habit is robbing us of not only of our hard earned money, but of our health as well. **The only real way to change this habit forever is to learn how to cook and eat without the two primary ingredients in all of these processed foods: sugar and flour.**

The No Sugar, No Flour diet was created to target this very serious issue. By eliminating sugar and flour, you are automatically setting yourself up to favor natural foods that are high in flavor, nutritional content, and complex carbs while being naturally low in simple carbs. The difference between complex and simple carbs is actually quite easy to understand. Complex carbohydrates come from grains and naturally occurring sugars that are found in whole, unrefined grains such as oats, barley, brown rice, corn, legumes, vegetables, and fruits. These naturally occurring carbohydrates take the body longer to break down, and this helps to stabilize blood sugar and energy levels. Simple carbohydrates, on the other hand, like those found in processed foods, provide a quick energy boost, but your body also burns through them quickly, meaning that you spend more time recovering and feeling fatigued, not to mention all of the other negative effects on your health. The best way to combat this is to learn how to eat while avoiding simple carbohydrates.

Many people don't realize that this is actually quite simple to do. Just because you are cutting out sugar and flour, that doesn't mean you can't enjoy grains or foods sweetened with the natural goodness of fruit.

This book has been created to show you that you are not missing out on anything by eating the No Sugar No Flour diet. In fact, you are opening up an entire world of natural goodness.

*Some recipes in this collection include honey or sugar free sweeteners. These ingredients are always listed as optional and should be included or excluded according to your personal preferences and dietary goals.

Honey is considered a natural sweetener since it is not refined like white sugar, however if you are watching your daily carb intake, you might want to choose a natural, carbohydrate free sugar substitute such as stevia.

Breakfast Dishes

Breakfast Polenta

Servings: 4
Cooking Time: 45 minutes

Ingredients
2 cups skim milk
½ cup fine cornmeal
¼ teaspoon salt
½ cup dried cranberries
1 teaspoon ginger, freshly grated
½ teaspoon cinnamon
1 teaspoon stevia or honey (optional)

Directions
1. Place the milk in a saucepan over medium heat. Heat, stirring constantly, until the milk is thoroughly warmed but not yet simmering.
2. Add the cornmeal to the saucepan and stir.
3. Next, add the salt, dried cranberries, ginger, cinnamon, and the stevia or honey if using.
4. Continue cooking over medium heat, stirring frequently, for approximately 15 minutes, or until thickened.
5. Remove the saucepan from the heat and coat a large serving bowl lightly with cooking spray.
6. Pour the polenta into the bowl and let it rest for at least 35-40 minutes, or until it is firm and set.
7. Gently turn the bowl upside down to release the polenta onto a serving plate or cutting board.
8. Slice the polenta and serve.

Nutritional Information (per serving)
Calories 150, Total fat1 g, saturated fat 0 g, total carbs 31 g, dietary fiber 2 g, protein 5 g

Sweet Potato Hash Browns

Servings: 4
Cooking Time: 15-20 minutes

Ingredients
4 cups sweet potatoes, peeled and shredded
½ teaspoon sea salt
½ teaspoon nutmeg
½ teaspoon black pepper
1 tablespoon olive oil
½ teaspoon thyme
¼ cup pecans, chopped
¼ cup goat cheese

Directions
1. Place the shredded potatoes in a kitchen towel or piece of cheesecloth and squeeze out any excess moisture.
2. Season the sweet potatoes with sea salt, nutmeg, and black pepper.
3. Heat the olive oil in a skillet over medium-high heat.
4. Place the seasoned sweet potatoes in the skillet, evenly distributing them over the surface.
5. Reduce the heat to medium low, cover, and cook for ten minutes.
6. Remove the lid and flip the hash browns over.
7. Replace the lid and cook for an additional 5 minutes.
8. Remove the lid and cook for an additional 3-5 minutes, or until crisp.
9. While the hash browns are cooking, combine the goat cheese with the chopped pecans and thyme.
10. Remove the hash browns from the skillet and serve each portion with a dollop of pecan goat cheese.

Nutritional Information (per serving)
Calories 241, total fat 11 g, saturated fat 21 g, total carbs 34 g, dietary fiber 5 g, protein 4 g

Giant Oat Pancakes with Ginger Papaya Compote

Servings: 2
Cooking Time: 15 minutes

Ingredients
1 cup papaya, diced
1 teaspoon ginger, freshly grated
¼ cup golden raisins
¼ cup fresh or no sugar added orange juice
¼ teaspoon cardamom
1 cup oat bran
2 eggs, lightly beaten
½ cup banana, mashed
¼ cup unsweetened shredded coconut

Directions
1. In a saucepan, combine the papaya, ginger, raisins, orange juice, and cardamom. Bring the mixture to a boil over medium-high heat while stirring constantly.
2. Reduce the heat to low and let it simmer for 10 minutes, stirring frequently.
3. In a bowl, combine the oat bran and eggs.
4. Next, add the unsweetened mashed banana and shredded coconut and mix well.
5. Spray a large skillet with cooking spray and heat it over medium.
6. Spread half of the batter in the skillet and cook until the edges begin to brown and crisp.
7. Use a spatula to carefully turn the pancake over. Continue cooking for an additional 3 minutes, or until cooked through. Repeat with the remaining batter.
8. Place the pancakes on serving plates and top with the warm papaya compote.

Nutritional Information (per serving)

Calories 312, total fat 11 g, saturated fat 6 g, total carbs 52 g, dietary fiber 7 g, protein 12 g

Baked Breakfast Brown Rice Pudding

Servings: 4
Cooking Time: 40 minutes

Ingredients
1 cup brown rice, cooked
2 eggs, lightly beaten
2 cups low fat milk
1 tablespoon chia seeds
¼ cup dried cranberries, chopped
1 cup fresh or frozen blueberries
½ teaspoon cinnamon
½ teaspoon nutmeg
1 teaspoon stevia or honey (optional)
½ cup walnuts, chopped

Directions
1. Preheat the oven to 375°F and lightly oil an 8x8 inch baking dish.
2. In a bowl, combine the brown rice, eggs, low fat milk, and chia seeds. Mix well.
3. Next, add the dried cranberries, blueberries, cinnamon, nutmeg, and stevia or honey, if using.
4. Pour the mixture into the baking dish and top with chopped walnuts.
5. Place the baking dish inside a baking pan filled about halfway with water.
6. Place the baking pan in the oven and bake for 35-40 minutes.
7. Remove the pudding from the oven and let it cool slightly before serving. It may be made ahead of time and served chilled.

Nutritional Information (per serving)
Calories 289, total fat 14 g, saturated fat 2 g, total carbs 32 g, dietary fiber 4 g, protein 12 g

No Bake Breakfast "Cookies"

Servings: 16
Cooking Time: none

Ingredients
1 cup dates, chopped
½ cup very hot water
2 tablespoons flax seed, finely ground
1 cup sugar free almond butter
¼ cup zucchini, shredded
¼ cup carrot, shredded
2 teaspoons ginger, freshly grated
2 teaspoons orange zest
1 tablespoon coconut oil
½ cup walnuts, chopped
3 cups oats

Directions
1. Pour the hot water over the dates and let them sit for 10 minutes to rehydrate.
2. Place the ground flax seed, almond butter, zucchini, carrot, and ginger in a blender or food processor. Blend until well combined.
3. Next, add the dates, the orange zest, coconut oil, and oats. Blend to combine.
4. Remove the mixture and stir in the walnuts.
5. Spray a baking pan with cooking spray and spread the mixture in the pan.
6. Cover and refrigerate for 30 minutes before slicing and serving.

Nutritional Information (per serving)
Calories 192, total fat 11 g, saturated fat 1 g, total carbs 22 g, dietary fiber 5 g, protein 6 g

White Cheddar and Asparagus Oven Omelet

Servings: 4
Cooking Time: 30 minutes

Ingredients
9 eggs
½ cup skim milk
½ cup light sour cream
2 teaspoons olive oil
2 cloves garlic, crushed and minced
1 cup mushrooms, sliced
1 cup asparagus, shaved
1 teaspoon tarragon
1 teaspoon sea salt
1 teaspoon white pepper
½ cup white cheddar cheese, shredded

Directions
1. Preheat the oven to 350°F and lightly oil an 8x8 baking dish.
2. In a bowl, combine the eggs with the skim milk and sour cream. Whisk together until smooth and set aside.
3. Pour the olive oil in a skillet over medium heat.
4. Add the garlic, mushrooms, and asparagus. Season the mixture with the tarragon, sea salt, and white pepper. Cook, stirring frequently, for 3-4 minutes.
5. Remove the skillet from the heat and let the contents cool for a couple of minutes.
6. Add the vegetables to the egg mixture and stir to blend.
7. Pour the mixture into the prepared baking dish.
8. Place the dish in the oven and bake for 25 minutes.
9. Remove the baking dish from the oven and sprinkle the white cheddar cheese over the top.

10. Place the baking dish back in the oven and bake for an additional 5 minutes, or until the center is set and the cheese is melted.

Nutritional Information (per serving)

Calories 297, total fat 21 g, saturated fat 9 g, total carbs 6 g, dietary fiber 1 g, protein 21 g

Spinach Frittata

Servings: 4
Cooking Time: 20 minutes

Ingredients
4 cups fresh spinach, torn
1 tablespoon shallots, diced
2 teaspoons olive oil
3 eggs
4 egg whites
½ cup brown rice, cooked
½ teaspoon salt
½ teaspoon black pepper
½ teaspoon nutmeg
½ teaspoon marjoram
1 tablespoon Parmesan cheese
¼ cup feta cheese

Directions
1. Preheat the oven to 400°F.
2. In an ovenproof skillet, heat the olive oil over medium.
3. Add the spinach and shallots to the skillet and sauté for 2-3 minutes, or until the spinach is wilted and the shallots are tender. Remove the skillet from the heat and set it aside.
4. In a bowl, combine the eggs and egg whites. Whisk together until blended.
5. Stir in the rice, salt, black pepper, nutmeg, marjoram, Parmesan cheese, and feta cheese.
6. Transfer the vegetables from the skillet into the egg mixture and stir.
7. Pour the entire egg mixture back into the skillet and place it over medium heat.

8. Cook for 7-8 minutes, lifting the edges gently as they begin to set, allowing the uncooked egg to flow to the edges and underneath the cooked egg.
9. Remove the skillet from the stovetop and place it in the oven.
10. Bake the frittata for approximately 10 minutes, or until it is set in the center.
11. Remove the frittata from the oven and run a soft spatula along the edges to loosen it from the pan.
12. Slide the frittata out onto a serving dish before slicing and serving.
13. May be served hot or chilled.

Nutritional Information (per serving)

Calories 152, total fat 8 g, saturated fat 3 g, total carbs 8 g, dietary fiber 1 g, protein 12 g

Lunch and Brunch Recipes

Smoked Whitefish Salad in Cool Cucumber Boats

Servings: 6
Cooking Time: none

Ingredients
6 medium-sized cucumbers, washed and halved lengthwise
½ pound smoked whitefish, bones removed
1 tablespoon prepared horseradish
¼ cup low fat ricotta cheese
¼ cup crème fraiche or low fat sour cream
¼ cup celery, finely diced
1 teaspoon stone ground mustard
2 teaspoons lemon juice
1 tablespoon fresh dill, chopped
2 teaspoons fresh chives, chopped
¼ cup fresh parsley, chopped

Directions
1. Begin by scooping out the center of each cucumber half to remove the seeds and create a well in which to place the smoked whitefish salad. Set them aside.
2. In a blender or food processor, combine the smoked whitefish, prepared horseradish, ricotta cheese, crème fraiche or sour cream, celery, stone ground mustard, lemon juice, dill, chives, and parsley. Blend or pulse until well combined.
3. Remove the mixture from the blender or food processor and spoon it into the center well of each cucumber half.
4. Serve immediately or chill for 2 hours before serving.

Nutritional Information (per serving)
Calories 157, total fat 8 g, saturated fat 3 g, total carbs 10 g, dietary fiber 3 g, protein 13 g

Cabbage Salad with Chili Citrus Vinaigrette

Servings: 4
Cooking Time: none

Ingredients
¼ cup no sugar added orange juice
2 tablespoons apple cider vinegar
2 tablespoons olive oil
1 clove garlic, crushed and minced
2 teaspoons crushed red pepper flakes
¼ teaspoon cayenne pepper sauce (adjust to suit tastes)
4 cups green cabbage, shredded
1 cup red cabbage, shredded
½ cup bean sprouts
½ cup carrots, shredded
½ cup onion, thinly sliced
½ cup broccoli stems, shredded
½ cup edamame

Directions
1. In a bowl, whisk together the orange juice, apple cider vinegar, olive oil, garlic, crushed red pepper flakes, and cayenne pepper sauce.
2. In another large bowl, combine the green cabbage, red cabbage, bean sprouts, carrots, onion, broccoli stems, and edamame. Toss to mix.
3. Add the dressing to the salad and toss to coat evenly.
4. Cover and place the salad in the refrigerator for at least 1 hour before serving.
5. Toss once again right before serving.

Nutritional Information (per serving)
Calories 140, total fat 8 g, saturated fat 1 g, total carbs 14 g, dietary fiber 4 g, protein 5 g

Polenta and Roasted Tomato Tart

Servings: 8
Cooking Time: 30 minutes

Ingredients
2 ⅓ cups water
⅔ cup fine cornmeal
1 teaspoon sea salt, divided
2 cups Roma tomatoes, sliced
2 teaspoons olive oil
1 egg white
½ cup goat cheese
¼ cup Parmesan cheese, freshly grated
2 cloves garlic, crushed and minced
½ teaspoon coarsely ground black pepper
1 teaspoon thyme
1 teaspoon oregano
Cooking spray

Directions
1. Place the water in a saucepan over medium heat and bring it to a simmer.
2. Add the cornmeal and ½ teaspoon salt. Cook, stirring frequently, for approximately 15 minutes or until the polenta begins to thicken.
3. Once the polenta begins to pull away from the sides of the saucepan when stirred, remove it from the heat.
4. Lightly spray a standard size tart or pie dish with cooking spray.
5. Spread the polenta along the bottom, making sure it is even and reaches the edges of the dish.
6. Cover and place the polenta in the refrigerator for at least 1 hour, or until it is completely set.
7. Preheat the oven to 425°F.

8. Line a baking sheet with parchment paper and lay the tomato slices on it.
9. Drizzle the tomato slices with olive oil and the remaining salt.
10. Place the baking sheet in the oven for 10 minutes. When the tomatoes are roasted, remove the baking sheet from the oven and set it aside.
11. While the tomatoes are roasting, remove the polenta crust from the refrigerator and let it come to room temperature.
12. In a blender or food processor, combine the egg white, goat cheese, Parmesan cheese, garlic, black pepper, thyme, and oregano. Blend until creamy.
13. Spread the mixture evenly onto the polenta crust.
14. Top the tart with slices of roasted tomato.
15. With the oven still at 425°F, place the tart in the oven and let it bake for 15-20 minutes.
16. Remove and let it cool slightly before serving.

Nutritional Information (per serving)
Calories 84, total fat 4 g, saturated fat 2 g, total carbs 10 g, dietary fiber 1 g, protein 4 g

Peachy Chicken Skewers

Servings: 6
Cooking Time: 15 minutes

Ingredients
1 teaspoon cumin
2 teaspoons smoked chili powder
2 teaspoons coriander
¼ teaspoon cayenne powder
1 teaspoon cinnamon
½ teaspoon salt
¼ cup peach nectar
1 tablespoon lime juice
1 ½ pounds boneless, skinless chicken breasts
1 ½ cups onion, cut into chunks
2 cups fresh peaches, cut into large chunks
Cooked rice for serving, optional

Directions
1. In a large bowl, combine the cumin, smoked chili powder, coriander, cayenne powder, cinnamon, and salt.
2. Add the peach nectar and lime juice. Stir until completely blended.
3. Cut the chicken breast into 1 ½-inch cubes and place the chicken and the onions in the bowl with the spice mixture. Toss to coat. Cover and refrigerate for at least 1 hour.
4. Preheat the oven to 375°F and lightly oil a baking sheet.
5. Remove the bowl from the refrigerator and place the pieces of chicken, onion, and peaches on metal or presoaked bamboo skewers in an alternating pattern.
6. Place the skewers on the baking sheet and then place the baking sheet in the oven.
7. Cook for 10-12 minutes, turning once halfway through, until the chicken is completely cooked.

8. Remove the skewers from the oven and serve with cooked rice, if desired.

Nutritional Information (per serving)
Calories 182, total fat 3 g, saturated fat 1 g, total carbs 11 g, dietary fiber 2 g, protein 27 g

Orange Fennel Salad

Servings: 4
Cooking Time: None

Ingredients
2 large oranges
1 cup fennel, thinly sliced
1 cup red onion, thinly sliced
¼ cup pomegranate seeds
5 cups fresh spinach, torn
1 tablespoon olive oil
1 teaspoon orange juice
1 teaspoon lemon juice
1 tablespoon rice vinegar
½ teaspoon salt
½ teaspoon black pepper

Directions
1. Begin by peeling the oranges and removing as much of the white pith as possible. Slice the oranges into wedges and place them in a large bowl.
2. Next, add the sliced fennel, red onion, pomegranate seeds, and spinach. Toss to mix.
3. In a small bowl, combine the olive oil, orange juice, lemon juice, rice vinegar, salt, and black pepper. Whisk together until well combined.
4. Pour the dressing over the salad and toss to coat.
5. Serve immediately.

Nutritional Information (per serving)
Calories 96, total fat 4 g, saturated fat 1 g, total carbs 15 g, dietary fiber 4 g, protein 2 g

Crab and Stilton Stuffed Avocados

Servings: 4
Cooking Time: None

Ingredients
3 large ripe avocados
¼ cup lime juice
¾ pound lump crab meat
½ cup reduced fat mayonnaise
¼ cup fresh chives
¼ cup Stilton cheese
2 tablespoons capers
½ teaspoon salt
½ teaspoon black pepper
Salad greens for serving, optional
¼ cup fresh parsley

Directions
1. Begin by peeling the avocados, cutting them in half and removing the pits. Brush the avocados with lime juice to prevent discoloration.
2. Take two avocado halves and cut them into cubes. Place the cubed avocado in a bowl.
3. Next, add the crab meat, reduced fat mayonnaise, fresh chives, Stilton cheese, capers, salt, and black pepper. Stir to combine.
4. Spoon generous portions of the crab mixture into each avocado half.
5. Place the avocado halves on beds of salad greens, if desired.
6. Garnish each stuffed avocado with fresh parsley before serving.

Nutritional Information (per serving)
Calories 282, total fat 20 g, saturated fat 4 g, total carbs 10 g, dietary fiber 6 g, protein 17 g

Roasted Cauliflower Coconut Soup

Servings: 6
Cooking Time: 30 minutes

Ingredients
3 cups cauliflower florets
2 tablespoons olive oil, divided
½ teaspoon sea salt
¼ teaspoon nutmeg
1 cup sweet yellow onion, chopped
4 cloves garlic, crushed and minced
¼ cup unsweetened shredded coconut
1 teaspoon curry powder
1 teaspoon basil
½ teaspoon ground ginger
3 cups chicken or vegetable stock
¼ cup unsweetened peanut butter
1 cup plain coconut milk
2 teaspoons lime juice
¼ cup fresh cilantro, chopped

Directions
1. Preheat the oven to 375°F.
2. Place the cauliflower florets on a baking sheet. Drizzle the cauliflower with one tablespoon of olive oil and season with sea salt and nutmeg. Toss to coat.
3. Place the baking sheet in the oven and bake for 15-20 minutes, stirring occasionally.
4. While the cauliflower is roasting, place the remaining olive oil in a soup pot over medium heat.
5. Add the onion, garlic, and unsweetened shredded coconut to the soup pot and sauté for 2-3 minutes.

6. Season the vegetables with the curry powder, basil, and ground ginger. Cook, stirring frequently, for an additional 2-3 minutes.
7. Remove the cauliflower from the oven and add it to the soup pot.
8. Next, add the stock and peanut butter. Stir well. Bring the soup to a boil and then reduce the heat and simmer for 15 minutes.
9. Take half the soup and place it in a blender. Purée until smooth and then transfer the puréed blend back into the soup pot.
10. Add the coconut milk and lime juice. Stir and increase the heat to medium.
11. Cook an additional 5 minutes, or until heated through.
12. Serve the soup garnished with fresh cilantro.

Nutritional Information (per serving)
Calories 225, total fat19 g, saturated fat 10 g, total carbs 10 g, dietary fiber 3 g, protein 5 g

Mushroom, Basil, and Barley Soup

Servings: 6
Cooking Time: 1 hour

Ingredients
1 tablespoon olive oil
1 cup red onion, diced
1 tablespoon shallots, diced
2 cloves garlic, crushed and minced
½ teaspoon salt
1 teaspoon black pepper, coarsely ground
½ cup dry white wine
4 cups assorted mushrooms, sliced
8 cups chicken or vegetable stock
¼ cup Worcestershire sauce
⅔ cup barley
½ cup fresh basil, chopped

Directions
1. Place the olive oil in a soup pot and heat it over medium.
2. Add the onion, shallots, and garlic, and sauté for 2-3 minutes.
3. Next, season the mixture with salt and black pepper. Add the dry white wine and cook, stirring frequently, until the wine reduces by about half.
4. Add the mushrooms and cook, stirring frequently, for approximately 3 minutes.
5. Add the chicken or vegetable stock, Worcestershire sauce, and barley. Bring the soup to a boil, then reduce the heat to low, cover, and simmer for 45 minutes.
6. Remove the cover and stir in the fresh basil.
7. Cover and cook an additional 15 minutes before serving.

Nutritional Information (per serving)
Calories 139, total fat 4 g, saturated fat 2 g, total carbs 23 g, dietary fiber 5 g, protein 5 g

Pumpkin and Black Bean Soup

Servings: 6
Cooking Time: 30 minutes

Ingredients
1 tablespoon olive oil
1 cup yellow onion, diced
4 cloves garlic, crushed and minced
1 ½ cups pumpkin, cooked and mashed
3 cups black beans, cooked or canned
8 cups chicken or vegetable stock
1 cup canned roasted tomatoes, with liquid
½ cup roasted red peppers, chopped
2 teaspoons salt
1 teaspoon black pepper
½ teaspoon cinnamon
1 teaspoon paprika
½ cup fresh flat leaf parsley, chopped

Directions
1. Heat the olive oil in a soup pot over medium heat.
2. Add the yellow onion and garlic. Sauté until tender, approximately 4 minutes.
3. Next, add the pumpkin, black beans, and chicken or vegetable stock. Stir to combine.
4. Now add the roasted tomatoes with any liquid, roasted red peppers, salt, black pepper, cinnamon, and paprika. Mix well.
5. Bring the soup to a low boil, stir, and reduce the heat to low.
6. Cover and simmer for 15-20 minutes before serving.
7. Add fresh chopped parsley before serving to each bowl

Nutritional Information (per serving)
Calories 138, total fat 4 g, saturated fat 2 g, total carbs 22 g, dietary fiber 7 g, protein 7 g

Oyster Mushroom and Chicken Stir Fry

Servings: 4
Cooking Time: 20 minutes

Ingredients

¼ cup chicken stock
¼ cup reduced sodium soy sauce
1 teaspoon sesame oil
1 tablespoon rice vinegar
1 tablespoon jalapeño pepper, diced
2 cloves garlic, crushed and minced
1 pound boneless skinless chicken breast, cut into thin strips
1 tablespoon peanut oil
2 cups oyster mushrooms, sliced
½ cup scallions, sliced
6 cups fresh spinach, torn
4 cups cooked brown rice for serving

Directions

1. In a large bowl, combine the chicken stock, reduced sodium soy sauce, sesame oil, rice vinegar, jalapeño pepper, and garlic. Whisk together.
2. Add the chicken strips to the bowl and toss to coat evenly. Cover and place in the refrigerator for at least 30 minutes, or up to 4 hours, to marinate.
3. Place the peanut oil in a large skillet over medium heat.
4. Remove the chicken from the marinade (set the marinade aside) and place the chicken in the skillet. Cook until it is evenly browned.
5. Add the mushrooms and scallions and sauté for 2-3 minutes.

6. Next, add the remaining marinade. Bring the liquid to a boil for 1-2 minutes and then reduce the heat and let the sauce simmer for at least 5 minutes, or until slightly reduced and thickened.
7. Stir in the spinach, and heat until it is wilted.
8. Serve immediately over cooked brown rice.

Nutritional Information (per serving)
Calories 410, total fat 9 g, saturated fat 2 g, total carbs 49 g, dietary fiber 5 g, protein 33 g

Crustless Spinach Pie

Servings: 6
Cooking Time: 45 minutes

Ingredients
2 (10 ounce) packages frozen spinach, thawed
1 tablespoon olive oil
½ cup yellow onion, diced
3 cloves garlic, crushed and minced
1 cup feta cheese
3 egg whites
2 cups low fat ricotta cheese
1 teaspoon salt
1 teaspoon black pepper
1 teaspoon nutmeg
½ teaspoon paprika
¼ cup pine nuts

Directions
1. Preheat the oven to 350°F and lightly oil a standard size pie dish.
2. Place the spinach in a kitchen towel or cheesecloth and squeeze out as much excess moisture as possible.
3. Heat the olive oil in a skillet over medium heat. Add the onion and garlic and sauté for 3-4 minutes.
4. Place the onion mixture, along with the feta cheese, in a food processor and pulse until mixed.
5. Next, add the egg whites, ricotta cheese, spinach, salt, black pepper, nutmeg, paprika, and pine nuts. Blend until thoroughly mixed.
6. Pour the mixture into the prepared pie dish.
7. Place the pie dish in the oven and bake for 40-45 minutes, or until the pie is set in the center.
8. Let it cool slightly before slicing and serving.

9. May be served hot or cold.

Nutritional Information (per serving)

Calories 262, total fat 17 g, saturated fat 8 g, total carbs 11 g, dietary fiber 3 g, protein 18 g

Dinner Recipes

Coconut Pecan Crusted Chicken

Servings: 4
Cooking Time: 30 minutes

Ingredients
½ cup buttermilk
1 tablespoon Dijon mustard
1 pound boneless skinless chicken breasts
½ cup pecan pieces
½ cup unsweetened shredded coconut
1 tablespoon fresh thyme
½ teaspoon salt
½ teaspoon coarse ground black pepper

Directions
1. Combine the buttermilk and the Dijon mustard in a large bowl. Add the chicken and let it soak for at least 15 minutes, but preferably for at least 1 hour.
2. Preheat the oven to 400°F and lightly oil a baking sheet.
3. Place the pecans, unsweetened shredded coconut and fresh thyme in a blender or food processor. Pulse until a coarse meal is formed.
4. Remove the chicken from the buttermilk and season it with the salt and black pepper.
5. Coat each piece with the pecan mixture, using your hands to pat it on if necessary.
6. Place the chicken on the baking sheet and then in the oven.
7. Bake for 30-35 minutes, or until the chicken juices run clear.

Nutritional Information (per serving)
Calories 302, total fat 19 g, saturated fat 6 g, total carbs 6 g, dietary fiber 2 g, protein 29 g

Spiky Meatballs with Simple Tomato Sauce

Servings: 6
Cooking Time: 45 minutes

Ingredients
1 pound lean ground beef
2 egg whites
2 cups cooked brown rice
2 cloves garlic, crushed and minced
2 (28 ounce) cans fire roasted tomatoes with liquid
¼ cup fresh basil, chopped
1 teaspoon dried oregano
½ teaspoon cinnamon
1 teaspoon salt
1 teaspoon black pepper
¼ cup fresh grated Parmesan

Directions
1. In a bowl, combine the ground beef, egg whites, cooked brown rice, and garlic. Use your hands to combine the mixture until thoroughly mixed.
2. Form the meat mixture into golf ball sized balls and set aside.
3. In a large, deep skillet, combine the fire roasted tomatoes, fresh basil, oregano, cinnamon, salt, and black pepper.
4. Bring the sauce to a boil over medium-high heat, and then reduce the heat to low and simmer for 15 minutes.
5. After 15 minutes, add the meatballs to the simmering sauce. Cover and cook for 30 minutes, stirring occasionally.
6. Remove the pan from the heat and sprinkle the Parmesan cheese over the top before serving.

Nutritional Information (per serving)
Calories 327, total fat 18 g, saturated fat 7 g, total carbs 23 g, dietary fiber 3 g, protein 19 g

Red Roasted Chicken

Servings: 4
Cooking Time: 1 ½ hours

Ingredients
1 roasting chicken, approximately 3-4 pounds
1 whole lemon, cut into quarters
¼ cup chipotle peppers in adobo sauce
1 tablespoon chili powder
2 teaspoons paprika
1 teaspoon cumin
1 teaspoon coriander
1 teaspoon salt
1 teaspoon coarse ground black pepper

Directions
1. Prepare the chicken for roasting by removing any chicken parts from the cavity. Place the cut up lemon into the cavity of the chicken.
2. Preheat the oven to 425°F.
3. Place the chipotle peppers with the sauce, chili powder, paprika, cumin, coriander, salt, and black pepper in a blender and blend until smooth.
4. Using a pastry brush or your hand, liberally apply the wet rub over the surface of the chicken, making sure to gently lift up the chicken skin and apply some of the rub underneath the skin surface.
5. Place the chicken in a roasting pan and in the oven.
6. Bake for 20 minutes, then reduce the heat to 350°F and cook for an additional 1-1 ½ hours, depending on the size of the chicken, until the juices run clear.
7. Remove the baking pan from the oven and let the chicken rest for 10 minutes before serving.

Nutritional Information (per serving)

Calories 281, total fat 7 g, saturated fat 2 g, total carbs 4 g, dietary fiber 1 g, protein 49 g

Chicken Moussaka

Servings: 6
Cooking Time: 1 ½ hours

Ingredients
1 tablespoon olive oil
1 pound ground chicken
1 cup red onion, sliced
1 ½ cups green bell peppers, sliced
½ cup dry red wine
½ cup golden raisins
2 (15 ounce) cans stewed tomatoes
1 tablespoon tomato paste
½ teaspoon allspice
½ teaspoon nutmeg
¼ teaspoon cinnamon
½ teaspoon salt
½ teaspoon black pepper
2 eggplants, peeled and sliced
2 cups cooked potatoes, peeled and sliced
1 cup low fat sour cream
1 cup plain Greek yogurt
2 cloves garlic, crushed and minced
1 egg yolk

Directions
1. Place the olive oil in a large skillet over medium heat.
2. Add the ground chicken and cook until browned. Remove the chicken from the skillet, making sure to leave the remaining olive oil in the pan. Set the chicken aside.
3. To the skillet, add the red onions and green bell peppers. Sauté just until slightly tender and caramelized, approximately 5-7 minutes.

4. To the skillet, add the red wine and golden raisins. Cook, stirring frequently until the wine reduces by about half.
5. Next, add the stewed tomatoes, tomato paste, allspice, nutmeg, cinnamon, salt and black pepper.
6. Add the ground chicken back into the skillet, cover and simmer for 1 hour or until thickened.
7. Preheat the oven to 400°F and line a baking sheet with aluminum foil.
8. Take the slices of eggplant, place them on the baking sheet and brush them lightly with olive oil.
9. Place the eggplant in the oven and roast for 20 minutes or until firm tender.
10. Lightly oil a large baking dish.
11. Layer half of the eggplant slices in the baking dish.
12. Follow this by layering half of the cooked, sliced potatoes on top of the eggplant.
13. Top the eggplant and potatoes with half of the sauce, and then repeat with the remaining eggplant, potatoes, and sauce.
14. Combine the low fat sour cream, plain Greek yogurt, garlic, and egg yolk. Whisk together until thoroughly combined.
15. Spread the creamy mixture over the top of the casserole.
16. Place the baking dish in the oven and bake for 20 minutes.
17. Remove the baking dish from the oven and let it rest for 15 minutes before serving.

Nutritional Information (per serving)
Calories 382, total fat 11 g, saturated fat 4 g, total carbs 44 g, dietary fiber 8 g, protein 27 g

Spinach Pie Meatloaf

Servings: 6
Cooking Time: 1 hour

Ingredients
½ pound ground pork
1 pound lean ground beef
2 egg whites
1 cup oats, coarsely ground
¼ cup shallots, diced
2 cloves garlic, crushed and minced
1 teaspoon salt
1 teaspoon black pepper
1 teaspoon paprika
3 cups frozen spinach, thawed, with excess moisture removed
½ cup feta cheese, crumbled
½ cup low fat cream cheese
1 tablespoon pine nuts
½ teaspoon nutmeg
¼ teaspoon cayenne powder

Directions
1. Preheat the oven to 350°F.
2. In a bowl, combine the ground pork, ground beef, egg whites, oats, shallots, garlic, salt, black pepper, and paprika. Use your hands to combine the mixture, making sure the eggs and oats are mixed in well.
3. Place a large piece of plastic wrap on the counter top.
4. Transfer the meat mixture from the mixing bowl to the plastic wrap.
5. Spread the meat mixture out onto the surface of the wrap to create a large rectangle.
6. Combine the spinach, feta cheese, low fat cream cheese, pine nuts, nutmeg, and cayenne powder.

7. Spread the spinach mixture over the surface of the meat.
8. Use the plastic wrap to help roll the meat into a loaf.
9. Remove the plastic wrap and tuck in the ends of the meatloaf to seal in the spinach mixture.
10. Lightly oil a baking sheet or baking dish.
11. Place the meatloaf on the baking sheet or baking dish and place it in the oven.
12. Bake for 1 hour or until the internal temperature reaches 165°F, when tested with a meat thermometer.
13. Remove the meatloaf from the oven and let it rest for at least 10 minutes before slicing and serving.

Nutritional Information (per serving)
Calories 468, total fat 31 g, saturated fat 13 g, total carbs 17 g, dietary fiber 4 g, protein 32 g

Venezuelan Tamales

Servings: 10
Cooking Time: 1 ½ hours

Ingredients

½ cup butter
1 teaspoon salt
½ teaspoon cayenne powder
4 cups beef stock
3 cups cornmeal
2 tablespoons olive oil
4 cloves garlic, crushed and minced
1 cup yellow onion, chopped
1 ½ pounds lean ground beef
½ pound pork, cooked and shredded
¼ cup capers
1 teaspoon salt
1 teaspoon black pepper
1 teaspoon paprika
1 teaspoon crushed red pepper flakes
¼ cup red wine vinegar
2 cups tomatoes, chopped
¼ cup fresh parsley, chopped

Directions

1. In a large soup pan or stock pot, combine the butter, salt, cayenne powder, and beef stock. Bring the liquid to a boil over medium high heat.
2. Reduce the heat to low and stir in the cornmeal. Cook, stirring frequently, until thickened, approximately 15 minutes. Remove the cornmeal from the heat and set it aside to cool.
3. Meanwhile, warm the olive oil in a large skillet over medium heat.

4. Add the garlic and onion. Cook, stirring frequently, for 3-4 minutes.
5. Next, add the ground beef and cook until browned.
6. Add the cooked, shredded pork to the skillet, along with the capers, salt, black pepper, paprika, crushed red pepper flakes, red wine vinegar, tomatoes, and parsley.
7. Cook, stirring frequently for 15 minutes.
8. Bring a stock pot, filled at least halfway with water, to a boil.
9. Lay out twenty 8x8 inch squares of aluminum foil.
10. Take a walnut-sized portion of the cornmeal and place it in the center of each square of foil.
11. Spread the cornmeal out into a strip that measures approximately 5x2 inches and is ¼-inch thick.
12. Spoon the sauce mixture into the center of each strip and press it gently into the cornmeal.
13. Take another small portion of the cornmeal and spread it out over the top of the filling. Gently press in the ends of the cornmeal to seal.
14. Bring the long edges of the foil up over the tamale.
15. Fold the edges over themselves repeatedly until they touch the surface of the tamale. Next, take the short ends, twist them and fold them under the tamale to seal tightly.
16. Repeat with the remaining foil squares.
17. Place the foil packets in the pot of boiling water and cook for 1 hour.
18. Carefully remove the tamales from the water and let them cool enough to handle before unwrapping and serving.

Nutritional Information (per serving)
Calories 501, total fat 32 g, saturated fat 14 g, total carbs 31 g, dietary fiber 3 g, protein 23 g

Greek Lamburger Patties

Servings: 6
Cooking Time: 15 minutes

Ingredients
¾ pound ground lamb
½ pound ground turkey
¼ cup brown rice, cooked
¼ cup plain Greek yogurt
1 clove garlic, crushed and minced
½ cup tomato, diced
½ cup red onion, diced
¼ cup feta cheese
¼ cup fresh parsley, chopped
1 teaspoon oregano
½ teaspoon salt
½ teaspoon black pepper

Directions
1. Preheat a skillet over medium heat.
2. In a bowl, combine the lamb, turkey, rice, Greek yogurt, and garlic. Using your hands, mix until all the ingredients are well incorporated.
3. Next, add the tomato, red onion, and feta cheese. Season the mixture with the parsley, oregano, salt, and black pepper.
4. Form the mixture into six evenly sized patties.
5. Place the patties in the skillet and cook approximately 10 minutes, turning once, until cooked through and no longer pink in the center.

Nutritional Information (per serving)
Calories 268, total fat 18 g, saturated fat 8 g, total carbs 7 g, dietary fiber 1 g, protein 20 g

Pork Medallions with Sesame Greens

Servings: 4
Cooking Time: 20 minutes

Ingredients
1 pound pork tenderloin medallions
½ teaspoon salt
½ teaspoon pepper
½ teaspoon ground ginger
2 tablespoons peanut oil
2 cloves garlic, crushed and minced
¼ cup soy sauce
1 tablespoon sesame oil
4 cups fresh spinach, torn
4 cups watercress, stems trimmed
2 cups bok choy, trimmed and sliced
1 tablespoon toasted sesame seeds

Directions
1. Season the pork medallions with salt, pepper, and ground ginger.
2. Heat the peanut oil in a large skillet over medium heat.
3. Add the garlic and the pork to the skillet and cook until the pork is browned, approximately 3-4 minutes per side.
4. Next, add the soy sauce, sesame oil, spinach, watercress, and bok choy. Cook, stirring frequently, for 5 minutes.
5. Add the sesame seeds, cover, and cook for 2-3 minutes.
6. Remove the lid and serve immediately.

Nutritional Information (per serving)
Calories 340, total fat 20 g, saturated fat 4 g, total carbs 3 g, dietary fiber 1 g, protein 37 g

Pan Seared Whitefish with Caper Relish

Servings: 4
Cooking Time: 10 minutes

Ingredients
½ cup green olives, pitted and chopped
½ cup red onion, diced
1 cup tomatoes, diced
1 cup zucchini, diced
1 tablespoon capers
1 teaspoon lemon zest
1 tablespoon red wine vinegar
1 tablespoon olive oil
1 pound whitefish filets
½ teaspoon salt
½ teaspoon black pepper
1 teaspoon lemon juice

Directions
1. For the relish, combine the olives, red onion, tomatoes, zucchini, capers, lemon zest, and red wine vinegar. Mix well, cover, and refrigerate for at least 1 hour for best results.
2. Heat the olive oil in a skillet over medium heat.
3. Season the whitefish with salt, black pepper, and lemon juice.
4. Place the whitefish in the skillet and cook for 3-4 minutes per side, or until cooked through and slightly crisp around the edges.
5. Remove the whitefish from the skillet and transfer the pieces to serving plates.
6. Top each fillet with a portion of the caper relish before serving.

Nutritional Information (per serving)

Calories 262, total fat 14 g, saturated fat 2 g, total carbs 6 g, dietary fiber 2 g, protein 29 g

Tilapia Poached in Coconut Milk

Servings: 4
Cooking Time: 10 minutes

Ingredients
1 pound tilapia filets
½ teaspoon salt
½ teaspoon black pepper
½ teaspoon coriander
2 cups coconut milk
2 cloves garlic, crushed and minced
1 tablespoon fresh lemongrass, chopped
2 teaspoons lime juice
1 teaspoon lime zest
4 cups cooked brown rice

Directions
1. Season the tilapia with salt, black pepper, and coriander.
2. In a deep skillet, combine the coconut milk, garlic, lemongrass, lime juice, and lime zest.
3. Bring the coconut milk to a low boil over medium-high heat.
4. Reduce the heat and add the tilapia to the skillet.
5. Cook, turning once, for 7-8 minutes, or until the fish is cooked all the way through.
6. Serve with hot, cooked rice.

Nutritional Information (per serving)
Calories 434, total fat 15 g, saturated fat 10 g, total carbs 47 g, dietary fiber 4 g, protein 29 g

Vegetables and Side Dishes

Stuffed Eggplant

Servings: 4
Cooking Time: 1 hour

Ingredients
2 medium-sized eggplants
1 tablespoon olive oil, divided
1 cup red onion, diced
2 cloves garlic, crushed and minced
1 cup tomato, chopped
¼ cup pine nuts
1 cup cooked brown rice
1 teaspoon lemon zest
¼ cup fresh parsley, chopped
2 tablespoons fresh mint, chopped
2 tablespoons Parmesan cheese, freshly grated

Directions
1. Preheat the oven to 400°F.
2. Prepare the eggplant by cutting each one in half and lightly brushing them with olive oil.
3. Place the eggplants, cut side down, on a baking sheet and put them in the oven. Bake for 20 minutes, or until firm tender.
4. Remove the eggplant from the oven and allow it to cool enough to handle.
5. When the eggplant has cooled, use a large spoon to scoop out the insides of each half, discarding the center area that is heavy in seeds. Remove the eggplant until you have about half an inch of the eggplant meat left in the skin.
6. Place the remaining olive oil in a skillet over medium heat.

7. Add the onion and garlic and cook for 3-4 minutes.
8. Next, stir in the tomato and pine nuts and cook for an additional 3 minutes.
9. Remove the skillet from the heat and stir in the rice, lemon zest, parsley, and mint. Mix well.
10. Spoon the mixture evenly into each of the eggplant shells.
11. Sprinkle the Parmesan cheese over each eggplant half and place the halves in a baking dish.
12. Cover the baking dish with aluminum foil and bake for 15 minutes.
13. Remove the foil and bake for an additional 15 minutes before serving.

Nutritional Information (per serving)
Calories 194, total fat 10 g, saturated fat 2 g, total carbs 25 g, dietary fiber 5 g, protein 5 g

Vegetable Lasagna Casserole

Servings: 10
Cooking Time: 1 hour

Ingredients
2 large eggplants
2 tablespoons olive oil
1 teaspoon salt
1 teaspoon black pepper
1 cup red onion, diced
2 cloves garlic, crushed and minced
4 cups fresh spinach
3 cups ricotta cheese
1 egg white
1 tablespoon fresh chives, chopped
¼ cup fresh basil, chopped
1 cup low fat sour cream or crème fraiche
1 cup fresh mozzarella cheese, shredded
¼ cup Asiago cheese, grated
1 cup prepared pesto sauce
1 cup roasted red peppers, sliced

Directions
1. Preheat the oven to 425°F.
2. Slice the eggplants lengthwise into large, flat, ¼-inch strips.
3. Brush each piece lightly with olive oil.
4. Place the strips of eggplant on a baking sheet and season them with salt and black pepper.
5. Place the baking sheet in the oven and bake for 10 minutes, turning once. Remove them from the oven and set them aside.
6. Reduce the heat of the oven to 350°F.
7. Heat the remaining olive oil in a skillet over medium heat.

8. Add the onion and sauté for 3-4 minutes.
9. Next, add the garlic and spinach and sauté for an additional 3 minutes.
10. In a medium mixing bowl, blend together the ricotta cheese, egg white, chives, and basil. Set aside.
11. In a separate bowl, combine the low fat sour cream or crème fraiche, mozzarella cheese, and Asiago cheese. Set aside.
12. Spread half of the prepared pesto in a 9x13 baking dish.
13. Arrange a layer of the eggplant slices over the pesto in the baking dish.
14. Top the eggplant slices with the remaining pesto sauce.
15. Next, top the pesto with half of the spinach mixture and half of the roasted red peppers.
16. Spread half of the ricotta mixture over the vegetables.
17. Next, place another layer of eggplant into the baking dish.
18. Add the remaining spinach mixture, roasted red peppers, and ricotta mixture.
19. Follow this with another layer of eggplant.
20. Next, spread the crème fraiche and cheese mixture over the top.
21. Cover the baking dish with aluminum foil and bake for 45 minutes.
22. Remove the foil and bake for an additional 10 minutes.
23. Let set for 10 minutes before serving.

Nutritional Information (per serving)
Calories 348, total fat 25 g, saturated fat 9 g, total carbs 14 g, dietary fiber 3 g, protein 17 g

Parmesan Roasted Broccoli

Servings: 4
Cooking Time: 20 minutes

Ingredients
4 cups broccoli florets
2 teaspoons olive oil
½ teaspoon salt
½ teaspoon black pepper
¼ teaspoon nutmeg
1 tablespoon Parmesan cheese

Directions
1. Preheat the oven to 400°F.
2. Spread the broccoli florets out on a baking sheet and drizzle them with olive oil.
3. Season the broccoli with salt, black pepper, and nutmeg. Toss to mix.
4. Finally, sprinkle the Parmesan cheese over the broccoli and toss.
5. Place the baking sheet in the oven and bake for 20-25 minutes, stirring occasionally, until the broccoli is nicely roasted with just a few lightly charred spots.

Nutritional Information (per serving)
Calories 45, total fat 2 g, saturated fat 1 g, total carbs 5 g, dietary fiber 3 g, protein 3 g

Glazed Brussels Sprouts

Servings: 4
Cooking Time: 30 minutes

Ingredients
4 cups Brussels sprouts, halved
2 tablespoons apple cider vinegar
2 tablespoons no sugar added apple juice or cider
¼ cup sugar free maple flavored syrup
½ teaspoon sea salt
½ teaspoon black pepper, coarsely ground
1 teaspoon thyme
½ cup walnuts, chopped

Directions
1. Preheat the oven to 400°F.
2. Place the Brussels sprouts in a microwave safe dish with ¼ cup water.
3. Place the dish in the microwave and cook for 4-5 minutes, just until the Brussels sprouts are firm tender. Drain off any excess water.
4. In a large bowl, combine the apple cider vinegar, apple juice or cider, and sugar free maple flavored syrup.
5. Add the Brussels sprouts to the bowl and toss to coat.
6. Season the Brussels sprouts with the salt, black pepper, and thyme. Add the walnuts and stir.
7. Spread the mixture out on a baking sheet.
8. Place the baking sheet in the oven and bake for 20-25 minutes.

Nutritional Information (per serving)
Calories 146, total fat 10 g, saturated fat 1 g, total carbs 10 g, dietary fiber 4 g, protein 5 g

Kale with Beets and Feta

Servings: 6
Cooking Time: 15 minutes

Ingredients

8 cups kale, washed and trimmed
2 teaspoons olive oil
2 cloves garlic, crushed and minced
1 cup red onion, sliced
½ teaspoon salt
½ teaspoon black pepper
¼ cup vegetable stock
¼ cup feta cheese
1 cup cooked beets, cut into matchsticks
1 tablespoon balsamic vinegar
1 teaspoon orange zest

Directions

1. Place the kale in a pot of boiling water. Cook for approximately 3-4 minutes before removing the kale from the water and draining thoroughly. Set it aside until it is cool enough to handle.
2. Heat the olive oil in a skillet over medium heat.
3. Add the garlic and onion and sauté for 3-4 minutes.
4. Next, tear up the kale into bite-sized pieces and add it to the skillet.
5. Season the kale with salt and black pepper and cook, stirring frequently, for 5 minutes.
6. Add the vegetable stock and feta cheese. Cook just until the stock is warmed through.
7. Remove the skillet from the heat and add the beets, balsamic vinegar, and orange zest.
8. Mix well and serve immediately.

Nutritional Information (per serving)

Calories 96, total fat 3 g, saturated fat 1 g, total carbs 15 g, dietary fiber 5 g, protein 5 g

Pearl Onions with Herbed Mushrooms

Servings: 4
Cooking Time: 15 minutes

Ingredients
1 tablespoon olive oil, divided
1 ½ cups pearl onion
¼ cup dry white wine
½ cup chicken stock
2 cups assorted mushrooms, sliced
½ teaspoon salt
½ teaspoon black pepper
1 tablespoon fresh thyme, chopped
1 tablespoon fresh tarragon, chopped
¼ cup fresh parsley, chopped

Directions
1. Heat half the olive oil in a skillet over medium heat.
2. Add the pearl onions and sauté just until they begin caramelize in spots.
3. Add the dry white wine and let it reduce for 2 minutes.
4. Next, add the chicken stock, cover, and let it simmer for approximately 7-8 minutes, or until the liquid has reduced.
5. Remove the lid and add the remaining olive oil, followed by the mushrooms.
6. Season the mixture with salt, black pepper, thyme, and tarragon. Cook, stirring frequently, until the mushrooms are tender, approximately 3 minutes.
7. Remove the skillet from the heat and toss with fresh parsley before serving.

Nutritional Information (per serving)
Calories 66, total fat 4 g, saturated fat 1 g, total carbs 5 g, dietary fiber 1 g, protein 1 g

Roasted Chickpea Salad

Servings: 4
Cooking Time: 15 minutes

Ingredients
2 cups chickpeas, cooked or canned (drained)
2 teaspoons olive oil
½ teaspoon salt
½ teaspoon black pepper
½ cup plain Greek yogurt
1 tablespoon Dijon mustard
1 tablespoon prepared horseradish
½ cup roasted red pepper, chopped
1 cup celery, chopped
1 cup carrot, shredded

Directions
1. Preheat the oven to 400°F.
2. Spread the chickpeas out on a baking sheet and drizzle them with olive oil. Season them with salt and black pepper and toss to coat.
3. Place the baking sheet in the oven and bake for 15 minutes.
4. While the chickpeas are in the oven, combine the Greek yogurt, Dijon mustard, and horseradish.
5. Remove the chickpeas from the oven and let them cool slightly.
6. In a bowl, combine the chickpeas with the roasted red pepper, celery, and carrot.
7. Add the dressing to the bowl and toss to coat.
8. Serve immediately or refrigerate for 2 hours before serving.

Nutritional Information (per serving)
Calories 218, total fat 5 g, saturated fat 1 g, total carbs 34 g, dietary fiber 7 g, protein 10 g

White Zucchini Bake

Servings: 6
Cooking Time: 30 minutes

Ingredients
6 cups zucchini, cubed
1 cup sweet yellow onion, sliced
2 cloves garlic, crushed and minced
1 tablespoon olive oil
1 egg white
1 egg
½ cup plain Greek yogurt
1 cup ricotta cheese
1 cup Gruyere cheese, shredded
½ teaspoon salt
1 teaspoon white pepper
¼ cup fresh basil, chopped

Directions
1. Preheat the oven to 425°F.
2. Combine the zucchini, sweet yellow onion, and garlic in a bowl. Drizzle in the olive oil and toss to coat.
3. Transfer the vegetables to a baking dish and place them in the oven.
4. Bake for 15 minutes, stirring occasionally.
5. Remove the vegetables from the oven and set them aside.
6. In a blender, combine the egg white, egg, plain Greek yogurt, ricotta cheese, Gruyere cheese, salt, white pepper, and basil. Blend until creamy.
7. Pour the creamy mixture into the baking dish with the vegetables and stir.
8. Place the baking dish back in the oven and bake for 15-20 minutes, or until lightly browned and bubbly.

Nutritional Information (per serving)

Calories 216, total fat 12 g, saturated fat 6 g, total carbs 12 g, dietary fiber 3 g, protein 15 g

Scalloped Leeks and Potatoes

Servings: 6
Cooking Time: 45 minutes

Ingredients
4 medium-sized potatoes, peeled
1 tablespoon butter
1 cup leeks, white and light green parts only, sliced
1 cup low fat sour cream
2 eggs, beaten
2 tablespoons milk
½ teaspoon salt
½ teaspoon black pepper
2 tablespoons fresh chives, chopped
1 tablespoon fresh tarragon, chopped
2 cloves garlic, crushed and minced
1 cup white cheddar cheese, shredded

Directions
1. Preheat the oven to 350°F.
2. Peel the potatoes and boil them in lightly salted water, just until tender. Remove them from the water and allow them to cool before slicing. There should be approximately 3-4 cups of sliced potatoes.
3. Heat the butter in a skillet over medium heat. Add the leeks and sauté until tender.
4. Arrange the potatoes in an 8x8 baking dish.
5. Layer the leeks on top of the potatoes.
6. Combine the low fat sour cream with the eggs, milk, salt, black pepper, chives, tarragon, and garlic.
7. Pour the cream mixture into the baking dish.
8. Sprinkle the top with shredded white cheddar cheese.
9. Place the baking dish in the oven and bake for 30 minutes, or until lightly browned and bubbly.

10. Let sit for 10 minutes before serving.

Nutritional Information (per serving)
Calories 280, total fat 15 g, saturated fat 9 g, total carbs 27 g, dietary fiber 4 g, protein 11 g

Desserts

Ricotta Pie with Almond Crust

Servings: 8
Cooking Time: 45 minutes

Ingredients
1 cup ground almonds
2 tablespoons butter, melted
1 teaspoon stevia (optional)
½ teaspoon cinnamon
4 eggs, separated
1 cup ricotta cheese
1 teaspoon vanilla extract
1 teaspoon almond extract
¼ cup unsweetened orange juice
1 teaspoon orange zest
1 teaspoon ginger, freshly grated

Directions
1. Preheat the oven to 375°F.
2. Combine the ground almonds, butter, stevia if using, and cinnamon in a blender or food processor. Pulse until blended.
3. Transfer the crust mixture to the bottom of standard size pie dish and press it evenly along the bottom and partway up the sides.
4. Place the egg whites in a bowl and beat until stiff.
5. In another bowl, combine the ricotta cheese with the egg yolks, vanilla extract, almond extract, orange juice, orange zest, and ginger.
6. Gently fold the egg whites into the ricotta filling mixture.
7. Transfer the filling into the pie dish on top of the crumb crust.

8. Place the pie dish in the oven and bake for 45 minutes.
9. Turn off the heat and leave the pie in the oven while it cools down.
10. For best results, chill for at least 2 hours before serving.

Nutritional Information (per serving)

Calories 238, total fat 16 g, saturated fat 6 g, total carbs 8 g, dietary fiber 2 g, protein 15 g

Figs with Mascarpone and Cognac Reduction

Servings: 4
Cooking Time: 10 minutes

Ingredients
½ tablespoon butter
12 figs, peeled and quartered
2 tablespoons cognac
1 cup mascarpone cheese
2 teaspoons orange zest
½ teaspoon cardamom

Directions
1. Heat the butter in a skillet over medium heat.
2. Add the figs and cook to soften, approximately 3-4 minutes.
3. Add the cognac and stir. Cook, stirring frequently, as the cognac reduces for 1-2 minutes.
4. Remove the figs from the heat and set them aside.
5. Combine the mascarpone cheese with the orange zest and cardamom.
6. Spread an equal amount of the mascarpone mixture onto each serving plate.
7. Top each plate with the figs and a drizzle of the buttered cognac reduction.

Nutritional Information (per serving)
Calories 297, total fat 20 g, saturated fat 9 g, total carbs 23 g, dietary fiber 4 g, protein 1 g

Gingered Pineapple Sherbet

Servings: 6
Cooking Time: none

Ingredients
4 cups very ripe fresh pineapple chunks
1 teaspoon lemon juice
2 teaspoons ginger, freshly grated
2 tablespoons pure pineapple juice
½ cup plain coconut milk

Directions
1. Combine the pineapple chunks, lemon juice, ginger, pineapple juice, and coconut milk in a blender or food processor. Blend until smooth.
2. Transfer the mixture to an ice cream maker, and proceed according to the manufacturer's instructions.

Nutritional Information (per serving)
Calories 86, total fat 4 g, saturated fat 3 g, total carbs 14 g, dietary fiber 1 g, protein 1 g

Au Lait Chantilly Cream

Servings: 4
Cooking Time: 10 minutes

Ingredients
½ cup strong brewed coffee
1 teaspoon stevia or honey (optional)
2 egg yolks, lightly beaten
½ teaspoon vanilla extract
1 cup unsweetened whipped cream

Directions
1. Combine the coffee and the stevia or honey, if using.
2. Place the egg yolks and coffee in the top of a double boiler.
3. Cook, stirring frequently, over hot water until a thick custard forms.
4. Remove the mixture from the heat and transfer it to a bowl.
5. Cover the bowl with plastic wrap so that the wrap is touching the surface of the custard.
6. Place the bowl in the refrigerator and let it chill for at least one hour.
7. Remove the bowl from the refrigerator and gently stir in the whipped cream before serving.

Nutritional Information (per serving)
Calories 233, total fat 24 g, saturated fat 15 g, total carbs 2 g, dietary fiber 0 g, protein 3 g

Blackberry Banana Ice Pops

Servings: 4
Cooking Time: None

Ingredients
1 cup mashed banana
2 cups blackberries
1 teaspoon lemon zest
1 cup plain coconut milk

Directions
1. Combine the mashed banana, blackberries, lemon zest, and coconut milk in a blender. Blend until creamy.
2. Transfer the mixture to ice pop molds.
3. Place the molds in the refrigerator for at least 4 hours before serving.

Nutritional Information (per serving)
Calories 194, total fat 11 g, saturated fat 9 g, total carbs 24 g, dietary fiber 5 g, protein 2 g

Conclusion

One of the most serious issues with the average diet is the abundance of refined sugar and flour it contains. This is a natural result of years of dietary trends that have favored processed foods over whole, natural options. Now, we have come to realize that cutting flour and sugar out of your diet doesn't mean you have to sacrifice anything in terms of texture, flavor, or quality. In fact, your diet can be more amazing and flavorful than ever when you switch out processed ingredients for those that are wholesome and natural to your body and your taste buds.

This cookbook has been created to show you that you not only have delicious options, but that you can also be creative. Those two ingredients that you are giving up do not define your diet anymore. With delicious recipes like these, you are on your way to regaining control of your life and your health for the long run.

More Books from Madison Miller

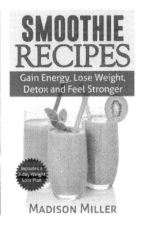

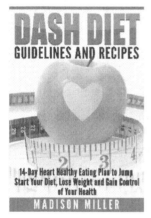

Appendix - Cooking Conversion Charts

1. Measuring Equivalent Chart

Type	Imperial	Imperial	Metric
Weight	1 dry ounce		28g
	1 pound	16 dry ounces	0.45 kg
Volume	1 teaspoon		5 ml
	1 dessert spoon	2 teaspoons	10 ml
	1 tablespoon	3 teaspoons	15 ml
	1 Australian tablespoon	4 teaspoons	20 ml
	1 fluid ounce	2 tablespoons	30 ml
	1 cup	16 tablespoons	240 ml
	1 cup	8 fluid ounces	240 ml
	1 pint	2 cups	470 ml
	1 quart	2 pints	0.95 l
	1 gallon	4 quarts	3.8 l
Length	1 inch		2.54 cm

* Numbers are rounded to the closest equivalent

2. Oven Temperature Equivalent Chart

T(°F)	T(°C)
220	100
225	110
250	120
275	140
300	150
325	160
350	180
375	190
400	200
425	220
450	230
475	250
500	260

* T(°C) = [T(°F)-32] * 5/9

** T(°F) = T(°C) * 9/5 + 32

*** Numbers are rounded to the closest equivalent

Made in the USA
Lexington, KY
29 October 2017